thicket

POEMS

thicket

thicket

MELANIE JANISSE BARLOW

Palimpsest Press
1171 Eastlawn Ave.
Windsor, Ontario. N8S 3J1
www.palimpsestpress.ca

Book and cover design by Kate Hargreaves (CorusKate Design)
Edited by Jim Johnstone

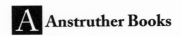 **Anstruther Books**

Palimpsest Press would like to thank the Canada Council for the Arts,
and the Ontario Arts Council for their support of our publishing
program. We also acknowledge the assistance of the Government of
Ontario through the Ontario Book Publishing Tax Credit.

Library and Archives Canada Cataloguing in Publication

Title: Thicket / Melanie Janisse-Barlow.

Names: Janisse-Barlow, Melanie, 1972- author.

Description: Poems.

Identifiers: Canadiana (print) 20190139978 | Canadiana (ebook)
20190139986 | ISBN 9781989287224

(softcover) | ISBN 9781989287231 (EPUB) | ISBN
9781989287248 (Kindle) | ISBN 9781989287255 (PDF)

Classification: LCC PS8619.A676 T55 2019 | DDC C811/.6—dc23

PRINTED AND BOUND IN CANADA

everything hangs damply in this parade:
conjurings

Triad. Everyone in sunglasses. There are Coca-Colas and lost apartments. I saw how the old gowns hung damply in the market. You visit with my enemies while my exercises do push-ups. You are too peopley right now. I saw how the empty buildings became full. You live in the corner of a condo, in a place where you can walk right up to the door. I saw how it was over between us, how the city grew overnight, how hiding has become.

My dog is pacing around me, silently charged. A fly bangs into everything in my kitchen. I think of Norfolk pines, but it doesn't matter. I use the deepest greens I have, but it doesn't matter. I am managing risk poorly. My skull is failing. My third eye is a cataract. I think of candles peppering a large deck behind an apartment building. New ceiling paint covering a long held smoking habit. I wipe up dog piss with spruce oil and hot water. My friends take me out for pizza at the Italian club. I maneuver through my isolation drills. Perfectly. With a devil between my toes. With a blanket over my head. It doesn't matter.

This better be true. When you say it that way. Lately my solar plexus is on a shifting plane. I am divided and craving. No one is getting back to me. My neighbor comes home drunk every night and wants war. We hold a candle to surviving. We are robed. When the switch tips, the dogs wait at the gate, needing. He dares me away, but I stay. None of us are ready to turn the light on, so we wait. The men are along the bar with rolled shoulders. Their hearts are crushing the beer mugs. It is too peopley here anyhow. We all gun our motors and wait for the start.

I have never wished anyone dead before. You are a memory of plywood floors. You win a shell of someone you made a shell. Congrats! Tie it up in your hair, bone bleached. Will you bleach your bones later? Late at night it stormed. I woke up short of breath but eventually it let up. There is no horror, just degrees of adjustment. Moonsets. I didn't win. You didn't win me over. Your skin is translucent and I see the waning of your blood right under. You are a beacon of lack. Panic and do exercises on your machines. I won't take it back. I drop the rocks and shells into the pot. Turn bones into gardens. I have never wished anyone dead before except you.

We fall. Dovetailing downward arcs. Cliff jumpers. He takes the scales off of his eyes, but only for one thing. I see a shopping cart on the street full of clothes. It is beautiful. I learn how to tie a Hermes scarf so it is tidy, it is beautiful. Norfolk pines are the right green. He has test jars full of small skeletons. Use the deepest green you can find. He has leek plants that are seeding and tough like you wouldn't believe. You couldn't bend them if you tried. We reach. Manage risk. Over there are the candles, foiling flame. It is easiest to make a fool of me. It is easiest to use the eraser when you ruin a drawing. Ceiling paint and candlelight are my flashlights. Spruce oil for fearless grace. Orange turpenades for washing away.

I walk around my studio in dirty feet. You are a Victorian novel right down to the stiff collar. A stalemate. Coffee. Cording. I binned the wedding cake you didn't eat. What I have won is sturdy in the spine. There are no bell jars for observations. There are four hundred different kinds of green, just in my studio alone. Jars of moss stacked up against mossy velvets. I am sorry, but you didn't win the prize. You won a shell of him that you made a shell. Congrats!

The corn is short this year. He calls once a year in order to leave his emotional work. He sends it in yard bags. He tucks it into my recycling. On all of the other days, it is quiet. My lilies are having problems, or at least a dormant year. I have been stuck since mid-June. It is irrational and the odds are stacked in the compost. I email him back his emotional work as dancing leaves, tell-tales, a case of mites. He probably will not understand, what with his liver spots and Florida tan.

There are helpers who don't help. It is for your own good, he says. I say it is for what you imagine my own good to be. You have always been wrong. I played Joni Mitchell the whole plane ride home. Today I will have a thousand awkward conversations about my own room. A time will come for fiddleheads, stewed peaches on ice cream. A time will come when the regime of you will end. Until then, the local yellow zucchinis are sweet. Until then, those who understand manage each other's risk.

Sitting in the Bronx Bar in Detroit, eating a BLT and waiting. Thickets. 1930's wallpaper inked with graffiti pen. The bartender tells me that John Sinclair still comes in sometimes and I remember a different version of me that used to care. Lately I have been playing Robyn Hitchcock on repeat in my studio. Osiris, transformer.

Trees are making their white noise heard. I see greens and whites on Egyptian brick. I see it my way completely. The sweet monk on YouTube gives my monkey mind a job. Watch the breath. I watch as it struggles through my throat, narrowing. I keep myself in an amusement park, regardless. The greens out my window capture this heartbeat. Diaphragm awry and dealing mutiny. My breath bounces from diaphragm to throat. A new plan is quietly launched. I bring my smoothie with me around the block. Put it down to pick up dog shit. Harm no one. Harm no one. I see it my way completely.

One of us is under the weight. One of us is underweight. Let's have a thousand awkward conversations. I am on the frontline of your skin. There is a key to a lock somewhere in my pockets. Let's have the smell of oil paint. Let's give it an enthusiastic review. The plants in the hall are my beacon on Thursdays. Let's lay in the quilt from the thrift store that we have shopped at forever. Yes, because our order is complete. We are captivated with what we captured. What are we doing tonight? Killing bugs? Crashing cars? What are we doing tonight?

You are welcome. You are welcome to borrow it. The measurements are off this morning but there are clean towels. A committee. We erase all signs. There are the glasses to attend to from last night. We attended last night but it didn't sway us. It didn't swallow us.

Each time I come, there are new spider webs spun in every window. Each ache increases with time. Locked knees and three pronged bites. Rain. Those who are edited out of the story are more interesting, and so I look for them. Old brass. Vaseline beads. Soon the boil of the day will come. Standing in the middle of a tack. Everything is happening around this body. This body is on tilt.

The city is a smooth assemblage. Rose hips on the pier pop with wasps while I no longer assemble. Those who assemble properly, make formation. I never do it properly, and so the gatekeepers are ruffled. Being 44 is punishable. I wished you were more courageous. We keep assuming the victim role. It is tiring. Let us repaint. The kitchen is tired. Walk the lake. There is a dedication each morning. Call the center itself. Exit each imbroglio with fewer tickets. Manage the hum.

There are hidden rooms in plain sight. Pass us over and we can slip back and forth unannounced. You can add embellishments. Take credit. We all lean into each other while sleeping. You are here but mourning. The heat has us restless, hangs across this morning. Waiting. Weight. Packages of cigarettes. Ears of corn. Ends of bread. You are wearing braids now. I am no longer popular. It doesn't matter.

notes for charliegirl: a long poem

NOTES FOR CHARLIEGIRL 1:

i

you announced that having dogs is too bourgeois& so i went to the
SPCA the next day just before i sunk the boat/ where the men fish
out the suckers/ it's all dogs in cones& dying hydrangeas over here&
i was sent home with different creams& shampoos/ but seriously i've
barely seen you since& what a relief cause you are no kind of friend

My husband insists on calling her Ketchup/ in hopes that she one
day will/ he says baby what is this violence that you brought home
today& now i love it/ this suffering/ i love this thing of suffering/
she peed on my jeans again/ how it constellates/ don't worry

i took her in after it was all said& done she sits on my porch a lot
licking her wounds/ i put her cone on& brace for the long winter&
the vet says that it is better if the skin gets some air/ so i try and take
the miniature tee shirt off but her legs move to itch as soon as the air
hits/ her tiny heart suffering in the meat

this problem you have is a deepdeep problem Ketchup/ settled itself
in seven layers from the surface of the skin/ cements itself in& i say
to him this is what you get when everything is suffering around you/
i saw this one laying there at the SPCA dying& thought maybe, you
know, just this once/ sorry about your pants

Ketchup's skin flakes onto the couch every time she scratches/now that the emergency is over& she can stand& feed herself/now that her stomach has stopped looking so minced& beside Ketchup on the couch my friend is tinselling apart words on her cell phone/the guy texts baby, don't worry jump over the ring on my finger& come party& i know that she will go/ why do i know?/ that's what comes to the surface when prodded/ at least along this dogged river/ it's the thing to do around here/ get your tattoos over here with me ladies& make sure that when the boys down here pretend to ignore you& walk around like these puffed up peacocks/ no wait that's the cirrhosis i think/ know what i mean?

i can't get with this/ neither of you are getting to the bottom of anything/ with all of your bloody picking at things/ your fits are synchronized/ you're both itching& real time healing requires rest& so when she goes to roll up her old forties dresses and fur hats& heads/ i wrap Ketchup in my old woven blanket/ that tiny head with all of the suffering bound/ i am blackhearted/ moss-gathered i sit there& wonder why the hell i feel so sick& its because she goes where some dude wants to settle his bullshit under the skin like Ketchup's mites& speaking of skin your work is showing me your self hatred& i judge you/ but only because you are scaring me into myself again

the lidcurtians of me/ the couchbones/ all of my messages are hued/ these infections/ this mass exodus& the mealy jealous tricks/ they insist on metrics that can't measure/ i can't measure the flail for the staying& equate any sort of solvency& so i just stop answering your phonecalls because i know that you will just tell me what i want to hear& continue& there is nothing i can do when the crotch of your jeans is stale cause you don't wear underwear& when the teeth are slightly rotting but you're good cause with some bright lipstick& some low lighting you know/ or at least i know& because of that i

am afraid/ each stem pink and looking too hard for a *party*/ fuck
Ketchup, fuck/ please get better

iii

when i went to pick up Ketchup at the shelter/ i met a father&
daughter who had come to retrieve a little white dog/ the dog's
mom& their mom& ex-wife was murdered on Bruce street last
month& the dog saw everything/ here is what i have to say about
fathers& daughters/ i nurse Ketchup to a place where she only has
outbreaks on her skin that are bad& this should tell you about the
first place

iv.

tonight is green and lowdown/ there has been a staff outbreak& so
you can find me mopping up this disgrace& shadowboxing bullies in
between orange juice& a cigarette/ you can find me hovering over
Ketchup& worrying about her ability to walk& everything in front
of me is stuck on repeat/ it's stuck on repeat& i say it real time/ i
absquatulate/ i am autonomous/ i can't get with all of this& i hear
that you went shopping for new underwear so you can go meet a
married man/ i hear they are sexy& yep its me again& they just keep
coming back firing up the skin with itch& Ketchup can't die/ she is
my only mascot

v.

i pull out of a sinkandfurrow/ tilt the boat back up cause otherwise/
doesn't it?/ is that what you wait for?/ holy Plath/ holy Sexton/
holy Smart/ holy MacEwan& i consider making a pin that says sad
lady poet/ i could start a team& when i first got clean i spent my
rent money on a pair of tiny brass moons from Gwendolyn's estate
because i heard she tried

tonight i put coconut oil on Ketchup's skin to choke the mites out/
LOOSEN YOUR HOLD YOU LITTLE FUCKERS/ someone
has to live here/ we right the boat the best we can& when they
finally go they leave the skin destroyed with infection/ make a huge
fuss as they die off/ she is laying on the couch& all i can do is give
some blankets as the winter hollows the stocks

NOTES FOR CHARLIEGIRL 2:

i.

you are sitting on my porch again& you narrow the Air Bnb search
over a tiny slice of Brooklyn/ make strange when i point out there is
all of Manhattan/ Flatbush you insist it centers your universe& the
subway lines suit your axis/ just in case

there are late trains that go further into Brooklyn you say& i say the
Lower East Side has vanished from the lottery somehow/ which of
course is where i needed to go?/ did you not know that it is on the
same subway line?& you hover your mouse fiercely over that tiny
slice of Brooklyn one more time/Brooklyn is some magnet

the Lower East side is burning/ it's a burning topic& its where i need
to go& really this is a tug a war between Brooklyn& the LES& really
there you are on my porch hearing nothing that isn't yours& who
really wonders why in the end

my husband left the hospital that day on Percosets/ bought some
underwear at the Winners on Queen Street while they stamped out
Gramercy as the fire had spread quite a bit& you could hardly talk
about my husband in the hospital because it wasn't yours?& here we
are fighting& Brooklyn is taking over my porch for fucks sakes what
about the Lower East Side?/ i like it there

ii.

lately i have been asked to use my words& i can't because its likely
that they will be switched around/ did you know that there are full-
time people working hard to switch my words to another whole set of
words that lean in another direction?& you assure me that i am also
making this up except am i?/ let me tell you about these entry points
of language/ let me tell you by using my words/ but in absentia&
outside of a counterfacutal reality if you don't mind

lately there are empty chairs at my ceremony/ just a few& its for the
best/ i am fond of the seven of Pentacles for its magical thinking&
amongst the rhubarb pies& gooseshit at the picnic i realize i tolerate
Mercury reasonably well

because i shoulder the load/ goat the road& what will happen if i
stop?/ i have noticed that my bank account is empty& its like the
vault of midnight around here so if you don't mind i will just keep
keeping on despite my fondness for the sadladypoets& our collective
recognition that it fits like a glove/ a glove i say!

iii.

the blossoms are out along Giles Blvd& temporarily bright in the
midlines today/ almost too bright but i like the candle of it anyways&
so i will consider it my blazon& follow the course/ put it all together
into one force if i can take it& i am never sure that i can you know?

last week i went& heard poetry humming in a place covered in
carbon/ somewhere on East Grand& where there was a huge fire
once& it's now in the walls/ it's now in the walls as they ricochet
poems to the best of their ability& let's face it they mostly absorb/ it
leaves me no choice but to burn our port sweetheart& so i fiddle for
the matches in my bag

NOTES FOR CHARLIEGIRL 3:

i.

my curtains are blowing out the upstairswindow/ screaming that my car windows are down/ i have grown accustomed to Rosemary& i am glad that she is back now& feeling well again& on her porch for small spells& back when i first got here my husband refused to return her husband's sailboat print/ they yell at each other about parking too close& threaten fists in the middle of Windermere as we watch from our windows& one day mine changes his mind& walks across the street with the giant frame& finds out that her husband didn't even want it anymore& did you notice after that they would say hello while unloading their trunks& ask each other how are you doing?

ii.

both the grandmothers died here in Windsor/ brittle boned& thumbed under& lately i keep picturing my nanny in a turquoise suit screaming BALLS at the top of her lungs in the grocery store aisle at the N&D/ lunges right out of her birded face& they were out of a can of something/ you know how it's the small things that send it out?/ i still have her tiny olive green clutch shaped like a half moon somewhere in my things/ her hair sprayed into gossamer& after church in the front seat having a hard time breathing anymore& back at home after the hospital/ an empress of birdladies/ piled up high in the bed down in the living room in a turquoise bed jacket/ satin/ amongst the crocheted blankets in blacks and beiges/ in the little west end house whose details to me are solar panels& a small garden at the edge of lawn& those shadowy kinds of rooms with plaid armchairs/ brown linoleum in the kitchen pretending to be brick& finally nanny had risen above it all like a little bluebird/ watching over her nest/ birding more towards her grave everyday after a whole life of disappointments you know?/ when she died we collected in a shadowy room at the top of the house/ the pitch of the roof& all of her things spread out on the bed by my mom and her sisters& there was something about the flesh colored underwear with support/ the knots of nylons& later on when my mother tells me about the time they were all dancing in the living room& nanny was laughing so much that she slid down the wall& peed her pants& it's how i want to remember her& them just busting out of the bullshit that encases& if my whole life is one resounding holler of BALLS! from the aisle over here/ it's for you

iii.

it is no longer just men that police me& this scares the shit out of me& so i open my body even further to you/ if it is the site of what you need& i will try live through it the best i can/ you need the airtime& i really don't so go ahead if need be& i am over here in my own meat/ i am a meat curtain operating the best i can& i think that i will pick up the dogshit in the yard today& i think ill/ i think i'll make the most of this halfway point/ i am working for free at this point for my own passage anyhow& i am running out of time& i think the stress test that women put other women up to is a shame& is about shame already& i am just someone else trapped over here in a meat curtain& i think i will have coffee right now& maybe get outside for a while if i can stand it/ the gaze i mean/ i feel like i have been put through a blender most days& so maybe i'll just stay in today/ its cool in here& nobody is looking at least

iv.

he caught a whopper of a halibut on the same day he mentioned
my ovaries were shut down by stage fright/ that's my family for you
anyhow/ the men minnow& bucket and wife& when i told you i
refused to be a piñata in a wedding dress/you found me anyways
with a big mean stick/ it's not that you are wrong it's just there is
just a feminism to my cantor& you must have missed the inference&
yes i quit the cigarettes/ *toxic little friends*& you pointed out a use of
inference that i missed but can totally see now& holy shit i couldn't
have nailed it better myself/ there must be a feminism to my cantor&
it wouldn't just be the truth would it?/ i told her that i was trying
to avoid being a pinata in a wedding dress& lo and behold& once
he told me that i didn't have children because had crazy women
all around me/ i wanted to point out that it was ok because i had
a house put aside for legions of yellow wallpapered queens/ but i
didn't get a chance because his vision of me was taking up too much
room& i killed the institution of family in one decision/ or was it
you?

v.

beneath my feet are hidden tunnels& bricked whisky runs/ my cousin
peeled these open on a spelunking dare back in the eighties/ damp
catacombs in his Nikes& he is still here washing windows& scraping
out leaves in eaves troughs/crisp sun strung sagging houses& houses
bombastic& statues/ wisteria houses/ houses near the casino are
like little cottages& tidy bungalows on the outskirts& he holds his
gaze under his Ray-Bans& i see him sometimes for greek soup or to
armourall my car

vi.

they say that putting your hands in the earth is a natural anti-depressant& so i weed one night/twinned dogs snore/ bark at the small street noises/ another dog five blocks away& honestly this has been a shit winter& honestly Ketchup is still a bit sick& when the storms come here they make the dogs tremble& the street floods into my basement/ there is always that& where the dip is in the middle of the street pools of rain water sometimes right up to your knees& my neighbors have cleared out their basement twice to the side of the house/ unearthed the broken up drywall in little white buckets& they start in with a trowel the day after/ i should know/ rain has a way with shaky foundations/ i picked you like a plum from all of this/ a ballast in my stormy sea& the anchor in a sea of talk

vi.

the spring brings hanging ferns& Canadian flags/ astroturf on porches where they watch television on laptops/ the smell of weed/ divided between those who inhabit the front porches& the ones that are never seen but have perfect arrangements for sitting anyhow& on garage sale day the guy next door barrels out his front door calling everybody BITCHES& threatens the garagesalers& the people walking to Art in the Park with jeers from his unloved concrete with no flowers& we promise to not tread on his weed-filled lawn& eventually he retreats back into his shuttered house/ the day carries on with face-painted children/ quarters and loonies piling up in the mailbox& my porch is artist turf& i wish to have my energy extend to its edges/ not like the trees on longbeach beaten away from the ocean/ growing sideways& bent through force/ i decide to grow two hibiscus plants up the side of the porch and carry on& if you don't like it/ don't look& Rosemary comes across the street heavy on the cane& missing part of her leg& survives the winter for the summer/ buys my mother's wicker chairs with the thin cushions and frills that

tie along the back& two of her plastic storage bins& my friends help
her across the street/ do her dishes

NOTES FOR CHARLIEGIRL 4:

i.

she used to be my friend, until she wasn't/ just like that a tiny little ghost story/ & its been eleven days trying to heal but lets face it i am still walking spine bent& how does one straighten up without losing what they were holding onto in the first place?/ lets avoid emotional dissatisfaction this Wednesday& remain silent at least until 6/ lets not mess with the pitfalls/ move across the sun like little dots/ hold a closed heart by hook or by crook& so help me god/ insist on the spaces between the vertebrae even when the damp sets in/ my uncle John died staring at his own belly button& it's not pretty/ so put on the chakra meditation its going to be a long winter over here

ii.

shroud the hook& when they take the bait aim low/ friends were at my porch like bees where you could hang like a tear drop in the hammocks last summer& those left standing will be the ones because i would rather four quarters than a hundred pennies& as i curl and fold into myself/ i definitely feel the grab in the meat as my heart hooks& i can't help but think of you too dead to give me away& my heart takes the bait once in a while when i find myself tired/ or hungry& when the angry& the lonely flutter around the edges/ i can see how you almost won/ captive in dreams& suffering in your meat/ i will roam with a want about the world& my friends fill the hole with keys to lighthouses& candles& cloth napkins& floating homes strung out in the middle of shiny white boats/ the ones that you like more than mine/ i am the poet in the old wooden boat& i used to stare out a lot at the spot in North Vancouver where Lowry lived in a stilt house/ impossibly

iii.

peonies are out& i pick them even though i know they don't keep/ nobody sits in the back garden filled with hostas/ just along the edges filling the ashtrays/ peonies are out/ think fast/ heartbursts/ tenderness unballing into papered joy/ silk cheeked/ tender heavy/ drooping groundwards& how the fuck do you open the heart?/ where does lift come from?/ levity where the spine grows long& the shoulders let go?& oh jesus the peonies are out

iv.

two cherry red shipping vessels floating together in a sea of ice blues are turning brown in west Detroit& the weight of this is a different kind of summer/ no knock on my door& i am still over here willing myself to believe in levity/ but i could just be rusting too/ it depends/ it depends& when the spine straightens i know that i have no loyalty to anyone& there is this vibration& i could be loyal to it/ it purrs like an engine hum/ the motor of this starting& i pulled the cord& caused my own combustion& what if i just got going& didn't signal/ does that cause harm?

who are you?/ this is me giving the dead away& the peonies out front have me on my knees you know?/ what if when i straighten my spine& drop the anchor/ the rope gets cut& my head springs up/ my throat reaches skyward& you seem to want to check& see if i am serious about all of this& make a bunch of noise/ make the room vibrate towards your own amplification& we all know it works to turn heads/or at least i do& keep the dress/ it doesn't fit me anymore& i drop these rocks& there will always be a woman who forces a room into the glove of her hand& gives over every damn thing to win the moment like a jewel& i just keep remembering the hollowed honeycomb of me in my own rented room late at night/

the candy rings of men's lips& a fading dress/ keep the dress& keep
the room& I am croning towards a quiet 45 minutes in my living
room on some cushions right now& the peonies are bursting out of
me

NOTES FOR CHARLIEGIRL 5:

i.

sometimes i get up in the morning& it looks like i am doing nothing/ it looks like i am simply laying there& the fact of the matter is i am trying to release something in my stomach/ something ossified in my throat& did you know there is a group of people in Japan that gather to do nothing as an act of revolution?/ i see you are still wearing my hat& if i could only shake this premonition/ Yoko Ono just tweeted out to *believe in yourself*& some solid part of me says yes/ you know?/ a grander vista has me on my heels& so i will lay here on my carpet for a while/ trying

ii.

i was talking to some friends the other day& i realized that i don't wish you well/ i don't& shame on me& i keep sitting here waiting for my solar plexus to offer up a blue building or a seahorse or an episode of Cheers& instead there is no magic unicorn that comes& unlocks what is stuck in me/ it seems I have a certain untimely commitment to this cause& every electronic device is plugged in& flipped on as i wait anyhow/ my horoscope tells me that my future will come on like a revved up engine/ stick close to home until I am complete& so i am pinned to my hometown like a dying butterfly& we are all challenged to see the real work week/ state our case/ pin our point/ threshold *iii.*

i am in a thread state for a thread which has not yet started/ do you feel well nourished& nurtured& supported& provided for?/ well no& it doesn't help that Francesca Woodman jumped out of her window because her funding didn't go through& my Fendi-wearing friends from high school are not seeing six months ahead& where is a thread state for a runnable thread/ can you google it?/

she took a running start at the goddamn thing& off she went/ all i see is a thread state for a terminated thread/ what remedy do you recommend when the sirens go off?/ Ketchup's fur has started to grow back& who's meeting up?/ my old best friend& the broker?/ the nun& the nurse's watch?/ kali, my bookkeeper& my checking account?/ things are getting prickly but moving quickly& my status bar is counting off& do you remember when i went through the dusty books in the middle of your floor?

iv.

sitting on my screendecked space-ship& there are pulsations that i have shoe-horned in between all the porches& there is a devil in my belly/ so fuck right off if you don't mind& if you don't give me room i will make my own& the same stray calico cat with a bit of mange walks her beat between houses& my dogs are at the window throwing a fit/ i want to hold your hand when you are old& say thank-you/ but i doubt it now/ i am no longer swayed by men with dental bridges& foxy shoes& since you might use the gaslighting card again& i am hungry for drama& i am lonely& i recoup *divinations*

DIVINATION I

Begin bawling bring forth phlegm in string-
a-lings toilet hoverer thigh-blossoms
of flimsy cotton making fugues breaking
cocaine peeling couches strung with cat
eyes chatoyant sternum jostles heart
homeward skyward cloud forms
your windows full of sycamore weeds run
to the sky ledges of tidy journals suck air
skin particles magical thinking. Clock ticks
begin meaningful positions shivering
cellulite dust bunnies drywall disintegrating
right in front of you pre-phoenix
queen of bitches broken arrows cuss me
out right at the corner why don't you
you guilt-ridden you know what
tape fifty dollar bills to my door on days
of crisis hang soft Portuguese bread
and deli meats on my doorknob. Crucify
me later

DIVINATION II

Staccato cigarettes snuffed in porcelain eggs
garbage a panacea ears corn crusts overfull
and you swear like a trucker take everyone
unaware and then there is the filth under
fur hats there are constellations strung
collarbones heading skyward strung
feathers but the costume jewelry weighs
you down just enough so you don't blow
away drink vodka blame the black shrouded
be a high-browed tough reed caught up in
elaborately groomed teaspoons
of sugarlemon tiny glasses of long dead
pheasants in the brushlight fires
sponge your feet on the pavement brim
bent to fit heart fisted spine

DIVINATION III

Textile sculptures of women assembled
at art school in the basement pausing
to inhale mixing spelt wheat soaking babies
with giant staring eyes from wooden chairs
pianos under the stairs blue like the sky
that day we left Montreal behind
New Brunswick fescues small pieces
of carved stone in your fingers. Settle you
into lonely Dartmouth apartments
with bleeding wombs lately we swim too
warm and crowded in Parkdale with Polish
women pervy men walk in the black cold
of High Park niveous ominous daring each
other to hold on remembering fluorescent
art school classrooms the black lights
in Montreal gay bars your black catsuit
and Fluevogs the guts to enter
the Lucien l'Allier metro at night, still
wondering why all of the bathrooms there
have windows that lead skyward
still thinking that if it weren't for your offer
of recipes that day or how you had to scrub
each and every plank of wood in the cracks
with bleach sometimes

DIVINATION IV

Lakes bookended batters and broths
inspissate in pots inglenooks book-ended
bursting loquacious nettles rose hips weed
drying somewhere as you teach me
how to rag tie my hair lend me socks keep
the chill off my feet amongst pencil
drawing ghosts. The mice keep eating dog
food creep around worn wood
those bastards you mutter lamprophonys
to lamplight with stiff night time whiskey
that slants sideways piss me off
but you are drunk singing like Rosetta
Parks so whatever. Moon flowers morning
glories souping kale skinning chicken
while farting wrapping your trusty shawl
set yourself down knead another pie
kindle another whiskey

DIVINATION V

Spend your nights devicefingered and lithe
with the noises around you forgetting
edit pictures of Darth Vader with a vacuum
a Día de los Muertos skull spread legged on
the couch spiderman kissing your son. You
use the paintbrush tool as he bangs pots
he runs around in Dufferin Grove Park
naked and mud soaked Toronto mothers
look down their nose as you drag away
at cigarettes divided slip through the crowd
like Francesca Woodman until you vanish
and we all look through the dark caves later
with lamplight trying to figure out
what happened what went wrong
with thriving

DIVINATION VI

Warming wax and tree resin between
your palms, coils of multi-coloured
string caught in the webs
of your daughter's fingers making
sense of the tangle, old wood,
old frames, falling apart on the walls
around you. These are your love
poems: coarse peasant wool dolls
in wooden cribs cuddled
into the crook of my neck, the blues
of baby eyes yearning towards me.
There are rows of paintings
dreams of cobwebbing oil paints
landscapes in the traditions Chiaroscuro
framed hats adumbrating
your Mexican woodcut old wooden
bobbins I promised myself I would not
resort to lists to describe your rows
that I would diffuse your natural order
with language break you apart
like your child's hands in the afternoon
everything she reaches a tangle
of curiosity you the cobbler
feather maker
mender
shining headlamps
blowing dust

DIVINATION VII

Glass trinkets tucking beer drinking
hipsters glass apples colored nicotine
a vegetarian dinner on a double decker bus
in Shoreditch then vanishing into the
morning clinking luggage down stairs
through the round parks with green shoots
and later iron railings and breath misting
cellphones yelling into the wind whipped
bridges earphones big and Detroit hip hop
with the curling cord because somehow
winning this fight is bravado still to this day
we try to win something here while losing
I crawl back into London town
from country hideouts sag paneer and
dosas thatched with aging DJ's
Canadian youth coming to a close with old
friends from Toronto whose children climb
over me like a hill

DIVINATION VIII

Hiding in the suburbs city receding
barriers built in round houses treed-in red
maples brilliant boughs dark wombs
quiet ticking rockers where he squirms
milky-lipped brave and beatific
smooth plaster wooden cathedrals holding
small dogs babies writing the quiet
afternoons of stewed tangerines bokchoy
nuts shortbread whispering in the sanctum
fugacious drives borrowed cars pinned into
maples into baby spit up hemmed in
by gentle sewing meaningful stitches
hold this in against dark wood walls
stone yellow marble moment priestess
in evanescent afternoons gossamer fall rain
and mouth full of every taste
strong tea the spider web of old teapots—
everytaste

DIVINATION IX

Captured in the throes of hipster regalia
cluttering heat score vans running
ever searching filling things up
filled nails for Christmas and couldn't
even feel the touch of this hometown
for a week filling the ropes of arms
inking obliterations of spaceship skin
filling to stave off the nights
toothpaste shed tangled brushes
on the bathroom floor makeup bottles
cream pots the bathroom floor a hot mess
wipe the sink with a piece of toilet paper
home town righteous mess of fisting
and imbroglios gossip making
camp across sparse wood floors
quieter still while working at these seams

DIVINATION X

Paper poem-strung people pleasing
fame seeking cynosures gather
an album crackling a studded leather jacket
lay it at your feet landlocked
in cheshires and children cheer
on the loud friend that distracts
your room for days old slips
serving the poems nodding to me
in neighborhood coffee shops
sharp children strung around you
in corn field hair remembering
how kissing you the night of your opening
it made me wet forget the corners
when the strollers stop the street
the sun moons

windsoria: the thick poems

The people here steal bicycles frequently and take all of the parking spots in their big trucks.

Their license plates that say things like 'Thirsty'.

I notice this as one of them tries to ram their front end up into my trunk on Ottawa Street.

On my dog walk just now, I found a dying hydrangea in a green plastic pot. It had been tossed into an old open trailer made out of wood behind someone's garage. It was just after I saw the bottle scavenger with wanker hair riding a tricycle. I told my dogs it was more his alley than ours, but they barked anyhow. It's a day to rescue tired plants and all other dying things I tell no one in particular.

I train my eyes towards rusty long dash in the river. It moves like a snail compared to the OCD, or is this anxiety? Either way, the lakers move. Most of the apologies are truly awful, but this one is hilarious.

Your secret beauty tip is a knife. What am I to think? People around here keep removing gates to the oldest of parks. Tearing down trees for a Walmart.

Here are some things that I do when no one is watching: brush my teeth in the shower, when I have them, eat things standing in front of my fridge, talk to my dogs while shitting. They always follow me in there.

We all hang on the wall, disarmed. At least my friends do. There are boxes full of mementos. My password contains a crying laughing.

The wedding beads at Dabl's are a commemoration. We pass like boats through Tuesday's social sphere. Watch our tongues and mind our manners. Ponder closets. Pull out delicacy. Balance balance. The friends that are on board find it hard to mingle. Do, do, do. Add more, more, more. Be at the end of the aisle, waiting.

I planted a hydrangea bush in my yard last week, but it just won't take. The leaves are turning a high waxy green have a yellow about their edges. I was bent on pleasing you back in the city. Now that I have given up on that city life it's all struggle in the dirt.

Devil-bellied we dig the exciting highs, challenging lows.

Pass me the museum of myself.

Words venture out, forking my tongue. Otherwise they just rest along the side of my mouth, nesting birds and wait for the perfect moment to resurrect. Cast your ballot against this working. Invest in estates of the realm. You know? This weaving eye sees mayhem. The poles are on tilt. Take refuge in reality, somehow. Live breathing, line the drawings. Pivot. Leave me with a lot and I will dig it.

Can I dig it? Don't tell me how it is perfectly legal one more time. Today I will exercise and make sure that I am only humblexcited, so as not to disturb you. I dedicate my sharing. Stretch on the dog fur car pet. One two three four. Boom. Introduce what is still true. Launch. If the sun is shining, I am consumed.

Last night, I saw a pair of antique stone lions on Kijiji. I thought of buying them, but without Bob Pedlar's house they don't mean as much to me. The guy who owns the place just stuccoed it this horrible gummy tan. Took the Gatsby right out of it.

All of these palimpsests somehow erase this place. This whole town.

Once the winter ended, I started to go outside. Dig at the snails in the back garden in their husky shells. I didn't know what else to do so I sent their little bodies over the fence and into the alley. In the basement, my clothes are becoming moth food. The dresses from Toronto that don't really fit anymore are covered in holes. Every time I go down to switch the loads of laundry, there are more pinpricks of light.

I have a quick glass of water with my gardening gloves off, wondering why it matters so much to me to keep the snails out, while the moths proliferate right below. Why am I getting fat? My pockets are filled with dog treat crumbs and there is saliva all over my coat from the two of them coming at me in the yard.

My low battery mode hasn't completely turned off yet. I don't have children. I do not tell children that I love them over and over. Last night I dreamt that flowers were growing out of my neck where my head should be. A pot of hydrangeas. The purple ones, the weaker plants that are only cultivated for Easter.

It's all better than nothing.

I think of all the woman poets I know, little pockets of rage and solitude. I remember walking around Toronto with a copy of Jane Bowle's short stories slotted into my bag. I took Jane out for an expensive dinner I couldn't afford and later I laid down on the couch I inherited from my last failed relationship and began self-consciously weeping. Lately, I am recovering well in the City of Roses. You reminded me that I had said that I wasn't loyal to anyone anymore. But you forgot the most important part. The next thing that I said was that I am loyal to some sort of vibration.

I joke often about my time with Bowles. The tissues that threatened to come up the sleeve of my cardigan. I do not like cats as much as dogs. I like fucking and good food. I like it when you have the guts to say things face to face. The silence down here is deadening. The porches line up in rows of lazy eyes. Turf wars take place in back rooms. How is everyone's middle class anxiety today? How are we all little islands of woman and poem? I am reaching out. I drove the 401 two days ago and the sun created suns on the face of every reed. Candled the ditches with poetry. I am in the market.

They keep finding bodies in strange places. Today it was a woman on a pedestrian overpass. Laid out along the ledge. This is a town where stores are robbed with machetes. So why was I terribly surprised?

Two women went into the river not too long ago. My friend's father was the engineer for the naturalization project just east of the site for both suicides. He was told the exact number of rocks that were to comprise each pile at the shore. Precise measurements to cultivate life right there. I will never have a baby tucked inside my sweatshirt like a kangaroo. There is a place I used to live where there was always a hawk in the sky. There is a tear in my eye in between sleeps. The snail contaminated soil was too much for me.

All joking aside.

I couldn't throw another one over the fence.

I am talking to the old love of my life, who marked himself safe from the bombs going off in his city in Europe. He has a new baby named Neptune, whose mother looks an awful lot like me. I think though, she might be better behaved.

Someone stole the hydrangeas I rescued the other day. Left the purple wrapper behind on the slope of my garage. I should have put those hydrangeas right into the earth, but right after I noticed them missing, my mother told me that they wouldn't take anyhow.

I stretch my hips out on the floor. On the carpet covered in dog fur and plan on drying my hair. If I am to write, may it come out freely like music or tangled like a thicket. A thin line of sentences. Life's missing ingredients. I have a friend on the West Coast who is hand carving runes out of found felled wood. One friend in the city wasting away with an eating disorder. I can count on Stephen to post photographs of nuns smoking cigarettes onto his Facebook.

It's not sexually interesting to me, just sadly comforting.

I behave exactly the same way as I did before. I ask one thousand questions to a lady with the visions. I drink my greens during weeks of sweeping motivation. Pepper it with coffees. Build sensoriums out of bathtubs. Highly curated with oils of lavender and cedar. Consider who might laugh at me when a show makes me cry. Somewhere a hundred people are gathering towards the waves on a beach. Someone is eating a lentil soup. Using some cheap perfume. Positive feedback helps. I am trying to dig out of a hole of sand. I don't know how to take the high road. Lately I have been trying coconut oil baths. I am in a tragedy of lost manners. I behave exactly the same way as I did before. You never come up on my porch anymore. No knock on my door. Hands are such tender meat lockers once they are aged.

It's always others who are more modern.

My psoas is hooking. Arches my lower back into an unreasonable mirror. The day I become a piñata in a wedding dress is the day i count missing seats. And when those seats split me open, you sing me a rope to hold onto. Our grey muzzled rat sisters heave and haw on your side of the bed when you are gone. I am an organized person. Where did I put you? What shambled pocket absorbed you? I don't technically need sleep, but the old dogs are itching on your side of the bed and it is two am in a bed of creepy crawlies. There is a bacterial infection afoot.

Are we eclipsing? Full mooning? Shall we put everything on hold until we feel better? I dream of the old days. I am serving brunch endlessly and the eggs are poorly timed. The brunch crowd is restless for some blood sugar. In the morning I coffee. Nip and tuck at some writing. The winter is waning and I assess my hips in a mirror, diminish the mourning.

don't tie the river down:
important postscripts

in it you keep trying to tie this river down

he knew who i thought i was, and so when you asked
he could clear
things up Charlie
girl

in it the dogs shit on the carpet again
always the same spot

he has a tiny straw skeleton that hangs from his
rearview mirror it gives us a hula wherever we go

in it a quiet shimmy

in it you are a real s.o.b.
she is never in her attic studio
in it we power wash the porch, julienne
the carrots also, we fuck all day on a new duvet

in it a triangularity
i collect Norfolk pines because they have stiff spines and soft
shoulders everything is up and down at the same time
the stars are explosions over Woodward
tonight we are all skinned and moonlight

in it the leaves get raked in it digested
psyllium compounding
in the intestines
scrapings near to the gut

in it twinned dogs snore
are moonlight i call them
my rat bastards
in it these two
snoring fur sacs
which remind
me
of balls

in it hanging ferns Canadian flags
astroturf they sit on their porches
watching television on
their laptops smoke
weed

in it turf divides

in it
it is so
tender, so so
tender
a heart
accordion
each chakra lighting up like a light
bulb
on the upswing
in it
a battle between
earth and water
interactive
Geminis in it
a cup of anger ferments
into a dangerous scoby we drink tumeric
until our mouths are a yelloworange
sweetsalty blend
in it
you are a dead giveaway

in it
an inner

pheasants on Brush street
scattering, multi- lingual the skirt of
Martha Graham evertwirling
in it gold tinsel swishing

an old, knowing
dog crouching
rusts
a tin ceiling bent

downwards in it

some kind of

holy order

two men in their cups on a beer-bottled
                        brown lawn
candles repelling bad
spirits

plants reach skywards old peeling
signs wilted text message tuning
forks, tuning

ladies dressed in white lining the
walls whispering
in it such an inner
in it the bricks are burning
we are eating garlic sauce and 3d pita in
Hamtramck with the sun kindling
in it those bricks are burning
the osteopath says my fascia has
become a sort of armor

in it my language opposites
in it i tell you to hang pictures of what
happened a productive Tuesday
in it problem solving is A1
in it i was thinking of tying a porkchop around my neck
so the cat would play with me

in it the stars are on an
upswing there was never a
first place
the a.m.

in it an inner
in it it is so tender
the winter hollows the stocks

in it such an inner
in it the big gallery wants to get with you

i am trying not to become a trope,
Charlie Girl a trope
throw some shade so you look
better don't mind me

in it a heart-accordion
each chakra lighting up like a light bulb on the
upswing in it a battle between earth and water

in it a man with one red nail picks
his nose outside of the Majestic
goes home with a drunk girl in cowboy
boots

in it a big black car that drives by us
smoking in it they will likely fuck

in it the porches are loaded

there are tubes of Paynes
grey
a bad poem
some hives along the jawline

never
come up on my
porch no
knock on my door
we are from the same heap
of salt ladies
someone come stoke these
rocks fire up
the air until it's so heavy that it smokes

in it all the objectioneers missed
the turn
the drunks forgot to leave
the bar that day

little birds are balancing on
basketballs and the ants are at the
melting

in it there are a thousand geese running through a long-grassed
field
in it a legion of ladies dressed in white lining the walls

pheasants on Brush street scattering,
multi-lingual the skirt of Martha Graham
perpetually turning
in it gold tinsel swishing

in it beersweating ballcaps
in it shade from the tallest building, casting

ferns against whitewashed concrete,
greening sky blue shirts, folded
tuning forks, tuning

in it

sippy
cups
wining
white dogs with fur
mats itching
plasticked
newspapers
hurling
leaky
basements
leaking
yards with
dogshit
melting

mind the words mine the inference dim the infertile tile the wood
fur the whorl hereicomehereicomehereicome there is a life after

stop measuring my sleeve Charlie,
because in it the men fish for the lost
ladies
in it that bitch of a river

in it there are long green plants reaching
skywards in it there was old peeling signs
a text message
in it candles repelling bad
spirits in it strings of sausages

in it these are not
poems these are
dead giveaways

inside
sweet salty
blend of now and then

you just gave me
an Yves St Laurent
dress a suitor gave
you
back in Hong
Kong his name
was Candy
he liked his cocaine

i wear it to a neighborhood barbecue in

Windsor in it an inner

an old, knowing
dog rusts
a tin ceiling bent
a black sweater with lint
in it some kind of holy order

in it a neon bathing suit
a steam bath
a neon bathing suit in a steam
bath pink neon suits steaming

in it two men in their cups on a beer-bottled
brown lawn red-fleshed, transported

perpendicular to the porch on a pair of
old chairs while they make me sad, they
are not unhappy there

they say that getting your hands in the earth is a natural
anti- depressant the anchor in a stupid sea of talk
i am trying to believe them Charliegirl,
trust me my porch is no longer your
sanctuary, Charliegirl it's no longer
cigarettes in the long afternoon, and this
is my loss?
this is my
loss this is
my theatre

don't measure my sleeve without my permission,
Charlie girl
my old best friend is my massage
therapist now
chips away at what has become ossified since we last saw each other

in it we are eating garlic sauce and 3d pita in
Hamtramck nowadays
drinking only moonlight

joining you down here by the water doesn't bring either of
us to mass have the dress Charlie—
i am getting too fat for it these days

in it my language
opposites
in it i tell you to hang pictures of what happened

in it the stars are on an upswing
this is a pearly white dashboard
only practical

in the a.m. i am entering into
a relaxed period, Charlie girl
thickening

NOTES

p. 15 references Robyn Hitchcock's 'Full Moon in My Soul' from the album *Spooked*. 2004. Yep Rock. In collaboration with Gillian Welch and David Rawlings. David Rawlings produced.

p. 28 'Holy' is in reference to Footnote To Howl, Alan Ginsberg, 1955, but also Patti Smith's recitation of this poem.

p. 60 'How is everyone's middle class anxiety today?' is borrowed with permission from a Facebook post by Nikki Reimer.

p. 64 references a work by artist Ihor Holubizky. The text is a play on the epitaph on the grave of Marcel Duchamp: 'C'est toujours les autres qui son mortes.' Ihor replaced 'mortes' with 'modernes'.

ACKNOWLEDGEMENTS

To the amazing team at Palimpsest, forever generous, kind and enthusiastic.

To my brilliant editor Jim Johnstone, for your skill, patience and generosity. For championing my work. For all of your guidance and friendship.

To Catherine Black for just about everything. My ballast.

To Faizal Deen for the genius of your feedback, your hammock visits, where we were poets together in the thick of it. You are a treasure.

To Phil Hall for believing in my words and for initial edits on this manuscript. For being an ally. For teaching me about poets in the thickets. For 1940's ties and deep wit.

To Pender, for long afternoons in poems, rollies, close reads and enduring with me. My bookend on Windermere.

To Lynn Crosbie for first publishing poems from *Thicket* on *Hood*. For your support and huge brilliance. For close readings and coming out of blurb retirement for me. For your legacy as a poet, for being punk and a lady, both.

To Lynn Crawford, for discussions of pheasants, for all of your support.

To Robin Richardson, who published first poems from *Thicket* in the mighty *Minola Review*. For giving space to women's words.

To all of those who took the time to read my work as I came out of a deep hiding to publish again. I am grateful.

To all of my friends, those who I brush shoulders with down here in the bramble.

To all of those who no longer orbit. Teachers of patience and compassion. My hugest lessons. Twin flames. Naysayers.

To my husband Andrew. My comrade. Ride or die. Deep love. Maker of magic. You are my way through.

To Patrice Mousseau. For all that you are. To Esme, sweet child. Goddaughter.

To my family who support.

To my beautiful nephews Matteo and Jackson. Breath and joy in the wilderness.

To Detroit, my heterotopia.

To all of the poets and artists, bravely holding space.

To Lance Dixon, Cindy of the Shoes, Pat Foreman, Billy Bryant, Gari-Ellen Brick, many others. For the keys of freedom. For healing.

To my pups Dimmy and Cher, who keep this writer company in the solitude.

To the Ontario Arts Council, specifically to the Recommender Grants for Writers for generous funding in support of *Thicket*.

To all who I pass in the fox runs as we travel. My kindred. Flames.

Melanie Janisse-Barlow is a poet and artist. Her first collection of poetry, *Orioles in the Oranges* (Guernica, 2009), was listed for the Relit Award, and her essay poems, entitled *Detroit*, were listed in Best American Essays in 2013. She has published in a variety of anthologies and journals in Canada and the US, and her painting practice includes *The Poets Series* (www.poets-series-project.com) —a popular portraiture series of contemporary poets, widely received and reviewed most recently in *Poets and Writers*, *Taddle Creek*, *The Humber Literary Review*, and *Quill and Quire*. She lives between her home in Windsor, Ontario and her wooden boat Kalinka in Toronto, Ontario.